University Life

A College Survival Story

WRITTEN BY:
TYGE PAYNE
JEREMY SHORT
ROB AUSTIN

ILLUSTRATED BY:
RACHAEL ANDERSON

LETTERING BY:
TESSA SHORT

FLAT WORLD KNOWLEDGE, INC.
1 BRIDGE STREET, SUITE 105
IRVINGTON, NY 10533
WWW.FLATWORLDKNOWLEDGE.COM

FLAT WORLD KNOWLEDGE, INC
ISBN: 978-1-4533-1014-

fwk-414034

D1307180

Not Just Comics: Or, Why Are Graphic Novels Valuable for College Education?

The term graphic novel is reserved for book-length works that are targeted toward adult audiences. Graphic novels are often used to convey serious, nonfiction content. For example, Jacobson and Colon (2006) published a graphic novel adaptation of *The 9/11 Commission Report*. The graphic novel *Maus*, by Art Spiegelman (1986–91), recounts his father's story as a Holocaust survivor in Nazi Germany. *Maus* was the first graphic novel to receive the Pulitzer Prize and exemplifies the medium's ability to convey serious topics. Marjane Satrapi's *Persepolis* (2003) tells the story of her childhood in Iran during the Islamic revolution. A number of graphic novels, including *300*, *V for Vendetta*, *A History of Violence*, *Ghost World*, *Stardust*, and *Road to Perdition*, have been adapted into feature films that also targeted adult audiences.

Graphic novels are widely read by college students, and in recent years educators have incorporated graphic novels into many university courses. Topics adapted to the graphic novel format include chemistry, genetics, psychology, history, physics, statistics, and ethics—to name only a few. The Federal Reserve Bank offers a dozen titles that are available for free to the public covering topics such as monetary policy, interest rates, and the history of money. Kaplan, a test preparation firm, utilizes the graphic novel format for SAT prep courses, and *Wired* magazine's Daniel Pink offers a career guide written in the graphic novel format. In Japan, it is common to see businesspeople on commuter trains reading graphic novels about business, and universities there have long used the format for teaching. *Megatrends* author, John Naisbitt, notes that the graphic novel is the only category of novel that is gaining ground in this increasingly visual age (Naisbitt, 2007).

Today's college students encounter and thrive on a vast array of stimulation and media input. To captivate modern students' attention, engaging and memorable educational material is needed. Graphic novels fit this need because they are visually appealing, concise, and unintimidating. We are pleased to present the first-ever graphic novel designed for incoming freshmen college students. We foresee this graphic novel being used for a variety of purposes. First, this graphic novel might be especially useful for freshmen transition courses. It would easily allow new students to familiarize themselves with key concepts and issues important to their success in college. The subjects and story lines developed in *University Life* are ideal for stimulating rich discussion and can easily be integrated into any teaching method in a manner relevant to multiple learning styles. Our graphic novel is accompanied by a full teacher's guide to highlight key concepts and questions, which will aid in the integration of content into the classroom. Second, we see this novel as a useful tool for focused orientation programs, such as weekend camps. Because of its brevity and innate appeal, orientation participants will have no difficulty reading the novel in a short amount of time. Finally, we suggest that this novel may be useful to high school educators and counselors who wish to create meaningful dialogue with high school seniors intending to go to college. *University Life* can be used as a supplement to a more traditional text or as a stand-alone resource.

References:

Jacobson, Sid, and Ernie Colon. 2006. *The 9/11 Report: A Graphic Adaptation*. New York: Hill and Wang.

Naisbitt, John. 2007. "The Postliterate Future." *Futurist*, March–April, 24–26.

Satrapi, Marjane. 2003. *Persepolis: The Story of a Childhood*. New York: Pantheon.

Spiegelman, Art. 1986–91. *Maus: A Survivor's Tale*. 2 vols. New York: Pantheon.

About the Authors

G. Tyge Payne is an associate professor of strategic management and holder of the Rawls Endowed Professorship of Management in the Rawls College of Business at Texas Tech University. An award-winning educator, Tyge generally teaches strategic management and organizational theory courses, along with an orientation course for incoming freshmen. His primary research interests include organization-environment fit/misfit, entrepreneurship, and social capital. He has authored or coauthored numerous publications appearing in such outlets as *Entrepreneurship Theory and Practice, Journal of Business Ethics, Journal of Management, Journal of Management Studies,* and *Organization Science,* among others. He currently serves on the editorial boards of the *Journal of Management* and the *Journal of Small Business Management* and is an elected member of the Governing Board of the Southern Management Association. Tyge enjoys playing the bass guitar and participating in outdoor activities such as running, mountain biking, and snow skiing.

Jeremy Short is the Rath Chair in Strategic Management at the University of Oklahoma. He coauthored the first two management and entrepreneurship textbooks in graphic novel format—*Atlas Black: Managing to Succeed* and *Atlas Black: Management Guru?* His award-winning teaching includes classes such as Principles of Management, Strategic Management, Entrepreneurship, and Management History. Jeremy's research focuses on the determinants of firm and organizational performance. His work appears in such journals as *Strategic Management Journal, Personnel Psychology, Organizational Behavior and Human Decision Processes, Academy of Management Learning and Education,* and *Journal of Management Education,* among others. He serves on the editorial board of *Organizational Research Methods* and is an associate editor for the *Journal of Management.* He enjoys playing piano, guitar, ukulele, and mandolin and taking walks with his wife, Tessa; son, Jack; and rat terrier, Rupert.

Robert D. Austin holds the chair in Management of Creativity and Innovation in the Department of Management, Politics, and Philosophy at Copenhagen Business School (CBS), serves as chief executive officer of CBS-SIMI Executive (the executive education foundation affiliated with CBS), and also cochairs "Delivering Information Services," the executive program for chief information officers (CIOs) at Harvard Business School. He is considered an international authority on IT, innovation, and performance management and regularly speaks on and advises multinational firms in these areas. Rob has written more than one hundred cases, articles, and books, including *The Adventures of an IT Leader, Corporate Information Strategy and Management, The Broadband Explosion: Leading Thinkers on the Promise of a Truly Interactive World, Artful Making: What Managers Need to Know About How Artists Work, Creating Business Advantage in the Information Age,* and *Measuring and Managing Performance in Organizations.*

About the Illustrator

Rachael Anderson lives in Lubbock, Texas, with her husband, Josh, and their two cats. Her artwork appeared in the first Harvard Business Case in graphic novel format (*iPremier: Denial of Service Attack*), and her work surrounding a family business surviving management fads appeared in *Business Horizons.* She currently works at Robot Cowboy Studios as a cartoonist with her friends and colleagues. She currently has two projects in the works: a sci-fi time-travel adventure series and a web comic about knitting. You can find out more about Rachel's upcoming projects and view her artwork at rleighsimmons.blogspot.com.

Your first year of college is often referred to as the "Freshman Experience." I remember my freshman year at South Plains College. I was an eighteen-year-old upstart who thought he could conquer the world; I was quickly proved wrong about that particular fantasy. However, certain important things happened that year that stay with me twenty-five years later. I took a philosophy class that totally rewired my world view; twisted my foot while playing badminton; fell in and out of love for the first time; worked part time at a secondhand music store, Ralph's Records; and went to an event that would later have great repercussions on my personal and professional career: I saw the Grateful Dead in concert (1985) for the first time, and this experience inspired my writing of three books related to the band (one of which directly relates to my career as a librarian).

But I digress—we are here to talk about YOU and YOUR "Freshmen Experience." Whether you are coming straight from high school, after working for a few years, or even if you have been out of school for more than twenty years, your freshman year is one of the most important and memorable times in your life. Whether you are eighteen or eighty, your first year in college becomes a milestone in your growth and development as a student and person. The freshman year stands as a basis for everything else that comes later in your college career. You may laugh, you may cry, you may even freak out a bit, or you may get your heart broken, but you will always remember it. The important thing is that you live and learn. You'll make mistakes and you'll have personal triumphs. The freshman year is a time for you to try to do your best and make an impact. Hopefully you'll gain some lifelong friends along the way.

Professors Tyge Payne, Jeremy Short, and Rob Austin have written a primer for the "Freshman Experience." It is a textbook to help you understand what you may expect and encounter during your freshman year. "But wait a minute," you might ask, "this so-called primer is a comic book?" (referred to in today's language as a graphic novel, or as sequential art, a term academics like to use to instead of comics). "You expect us to read comics to understand how freshman life works?" Well, in a word, YES!!!!!!!!!!!!!!!!!!!!!

Sequential art/comics have received a bad rap over the last fifty years. They have often been thought of as garbage literature, written for those with little or no intelligence, or as fodder for children. (The truth is comics were never just for children.) At one time during the fifties, comics were even accused of causing crime and juvenile delinquency. This "ten-cent plague" was seen as the worst kind of trash (similar to some of the same arguments leveled at video games, texting, etc., today).

Today things are changing in a more positive way. Graphic novel publishing is one of the few areas of print publishing that continues to grow year after year, even as we become increasingly enmeshed in the digital world and culture. Far from "dumbing down" one's reading ability, reading comics can actually make you smarter. Both sides of the brain are used when reading a comic. You use the left side of your brain to interpret the written narrative (or word balloons) and the right side to interpret the art/pictures. So reading comics helps both sides of the brain work together in a more unifying way.

The artistry of Rachel Anderson excels in presenting characters that are realistic. You become involved with the trials and tribulations they go through. You'll find characters that are not that different from the friends you have or people you encounter along the way: the characters go through experiences and situations that are familiar to your life as a freshman. The art just enhances the already outstanding script.

University Life: A College Survival Story is designed to be used as a textbook for a freshman seminar and/or Introduction to College Life classes. This graphic novel is also a vital addition to library collections of all kinds. Public, academic, community college, private, and school libraries will all want to have Professors Payne, Short, and Austin's graphic novel on their shelves. The writers, artistic team, and publisher, Flat World Knowledge, have done a great service to the college community as a whole. The topics discussed throughout this graphic novel are universal regardless of where you may be attending classes. There is something here for EVERY FRESHMAN to learn and gain from.

Oh, did I mention that *University Life: A College Survival Story* is fun to read without sacrificing content? Who says education can't be fun?????????????

Go forth, read, learn, and take an active part in your "Freshman Experience." BRAVO!

Robert G. Weiner

Robert G. Weiner is associate humanities librarian for the Texas Tech University Libraries. He is the author of *Marvel Graphic Novels: An Annotated Guide, 1965-2005* and editor of *Captain America and the Struggle of the Superhero* and *Graphic Novels in Comics in Libraries and Archives*.

University Life

A College Survival Story

Save Stuff!

CHAPTER 1: A FRESH START

BY DORM

REALLY, MOM, I'VE GOT EVERYTHING... NO NEED TO COME IN. NO, REALLY, I'VE GOT IT.

ARE YOU SURE YOU DON'T WANT ME TO HELP PUT YOUR CLOTHES AWAY AND MAKE YOUR BED? THOSE FITTED SHEETS CAN BE REAL TROUBLE.

AND THAT PROBLEM WITH YOUR SCHEDULE...

I'VE GOT IT FROM HERE, MOM. TELL DAD EVERYTHING IS GREAT, AND I'LL CALL YOU SOON.

I LOVE YOU, MOM. BYE!

I'LL JUST MAIL THESE, I GUESS.

SO, YOU MUST BE MY NEW OOMMATE, MASON CARVER? RIGHT?

HOPE YOU DON'T MIND, I TOOK THE BED BY THE WINDOW.

AND, UH, I'VE GOT A LOT OF POSTERS, BUT I LEFT YOU A LITTLE SPACE ON BACK OF THE DOOR. I MOVED IN LAST WEEK... HAD TO GET HERE EARLY FOR FOOTBALL. I'M TRAVIS HELTER.

UH, NICE TO MEET YOU.

WHAT'S UP, BRO?

THERE'S BEEN A MISTAKE. I'M NOT REGISTERED FOR A COURSE REQUIRED BY MY MAJOR.

IN A FEW MINUTES? I DON'T THINK I CAN GO TO THAT, I'VE GOT TO FIX MY SCHEDULE.

DUDE, YOU CAN UNPACK LATER. YOU KNOW WE HAVE A DORM-WIDE MEETING IN A FEW MINUTES?

RELAX, MAN, YOU GOT TIME. GOT TO GO TO THE DORM MEETING, IT'S "MANDATORY." WE BETTER GET GOING, COME ON!

ALRIGHT! EVERYONE! ATTENTION! **ATTENTION!**

EVERYONE! **SHUT UP!!**

BBBBLLLLLEEEEEEPPPPP!!!

HELLO, EVERYONE! AND, WELCOME! I'M STEVE, THE SENIOR RESIDENT ASSISTANT, OR RA FOR SHORT, FOR WELBY DORM.

THIS YEAR I HAVE BEEN PUT IN CHARGE OF THE OPENING WEEKEND ACTIVITIES. SO ARE YOU READY TO **PARTY WELBY STYLE?!**

UM, ANYWAY, YOU SHOULD HAVE RECEIVED A DETAILED LIST OF ACTIVITIES AND OTHER INFORMATION IN YOUR OPENING WEEKEND PACKET.

WELCOME TO THE GREATEST UNIVERSITY IN THE WORLD!!

THIS GUY NEEDS TO GET OUT MORE.

NERD ALERT.

WHATEVER.

CAN YOU BELIEVE THAT GUY? HE WOULD BE BETTER OFF IN A CHEERLEADING SKIRT. MAN, I'M STARVING. IS HE DONE YET?

OK, WELL LET'S HOPE YOU HAVE MORE SPIRIT IN A FEW

TIGERS RULE! ROAR!!!!

WEEKS WHEN WE PLAY OUR FIRST FOOTBALL GAME AT MACGREGOR STADIUM.

WASN'T OUR RECORD SOMETHING LIKE FOUR AND NINE LAST YEAR?

YEAH, WELL, WE ARE MUCH BETTER THIS YEAR.

SO, IF YOU LOOK AT YOUR ACTIVITIES LIST YOU WILL NOTE THAT

THIS AFTERNOON, EVERYONE IS GOING TO BE PLAYING IN A VOLLEYBALL TOURNAMENT.

YES, I SAID EVERYONE! TEAMS HAVE ALREADY BEEN RANDOMLY ASSIGNED.

THREE MEN AND THREE WOMEN. THE TEAMS AND TOURNAMENT BRACKET ARE POSTED ON THE BACK WALL.

I GUESS WE'LL FIND OUT SOON ENOUGH. IT SAYS AT THE BOTTOM OF THE LIST WE'RE SUPPOSED TO

MEET THE REST OF THE TEAM ON BEACH COURT #4 AT 2:45 P.M. MAYBE I'VE GOT TIME TO CHECK MY SCHEDULE THING...

ARE YOU KIDDING? WE STILL HAVE TO CHANGE CLOTHES, GET SOME FOOD, PUT TOGETHER SOME BASIC OFFENSIVE AND DEFENSIVE PLAYS...

WE PROBABLY NEED A TEAM NAME TOO, HUH? ANY IDEAS?

MAYBE, "MY ROOMMATE IS SO FULL OF..."

YEAH, OK... BUT AT SOME POINT I NEED TO.

WHAT WAS THAT?

OHHH, UMMMM, I WAS THINKING WE SHOULD CALL OURSELVES SOMETHING LIKE "FULL OF HITS"?!?

WE SHOULD GET SOME T-SHIRTS MADE!

I'LL GET RIGHT ON IT.

I WONDER WHERE THE OTHER TWO GUYS ARE. WE'RE SUPPOSED TO START IN 10 MINUTES.

I DON'T KNOW... BUT I HOPE AT LEAST ONE OF THEM IS CUTE. I AM NOT SURE HOW THEY SELECTED THE TEAMS THOUGH.

I AM SURE IT WAS RANDOM, SINCE THERE WOULD BE NO OTHER FAIR WAY TO DO IT. BUT WE COULDN'T HAVE PLANNED FOR AS MUCH BEAUTIFUL DIVERSITY AS IT SEEMS WE HAVE ON OUR TEAM.

UM, OK.

AND YOU MUST BE HEATHER, RIGHT?

YES, HEATHER SPILLS.

I KNEW THAT YOU WOULD BE...MMM, NEVER MIND...

ARE YOU GOOD AT VOLLEYBALL, AJEET??

NO PROBLEM!

SO, REALLY...HAS ANYONE PLAYED MUCH BEFORE? BESIDES ME, THAT IS?

THEN I GUESS THAT MAKES ME CAPTAIN!

I TOOK THE OPPORTUNITY TO DRAW UP A FEW BASIC PLAYS.

OH, BROTHER!

TEAM? REALLY? YOU CAN'T BE SERIOUS... A TEAM? YOU'RE HITTING EVERYTHING BEFORE WE GET A CHANCE!

I DON'T THINK MCALISTER HAS TOUCHED THE BALL YET!

SOOOO, SORRY! I AM JUST TRYING TO WIN! YOU GOT SOMETHING AGAINST WINNING?!?

NO, BUT EVERYONE DESERVES A CHANCE TO PLAY. THIS ISN'T ALL ABOUT WINNING, IT'S ABOUT EVERYONE GETTING TO PARTICIPATE AND GETTING TO KNOW ONE ANOTHER!

HOW ABOUT THIS NEXT GAME WE ALL PLAY OUR POSITION - AS A REAL TEAM!

YEAH, TRAVIS...LET'S GIVE THE OTHERS A CHANCE TO PLAY SOME...OK? IT'S NOT THAT BIG OF A DEAL.

ALRIGHT, HAVE IT YOUR WAY...BUT I BETTER SEE SOME HUSTLE OUT THERE.

HERE COMES OUR NEXT TEAM, "THE VOLLEY OF DEATH."

SPECIFICALLY, WE WANT YOU TO MAKE SOME FRIENDS WITH PEOPLE YOU MIGHT NOT NORMALLY HANG OUT WITH.

THE RAS WILL KEEP TRACK OF ATTENDANCE AND PARTICIPATION.

ALSO, EACH PEER GROUP WILL BE PLACED UNDER THE SUPERVISION OF ONE OF THE RAS.

THIS GROUP IS THE SAME GROUP YOU PLAYED VOLLEYBALL WITH TODAY, SO YOU SHOULD BE PRETTY FAMILIAR WITH EACH OTHER ALREADY!

SPEAKING OF TRACKING, MAKE SURE TO WAIT THIRTY MINUTES AFTER EATING BEFORE YOU TAKE A DIP IN THE POOL!

STRANGELY, THAT DUDE STEVE SOUNDS A LOT LIKE MY MOTHER.

MAN, I DON'T KNOW...I'M NOT THAT GOOD AT TALKING TO GIRLS. AND I'VE GOT THIS THING I'VE GOTTA CHECK...

DUDE, THERE'S HEATHER! LET'S GO TALK TO HER AND THEN SHE'LL INTRODUCE US TO HER FRIENDS!

AW, C'MON. IT'S JUST LIKE FOOTBALL. YOU PLAY LIKE YOU PRACTICE. SO LET'S PRACTICE, PLAY-AH. JUST STAY POSITIVE AND LET YOUR SUPPORTIVE WINGMAN LEAD THE WAY.

FINE. LEAD THE WAY, ACE.

LET'S GET STARTED. IF YOU DON'T KNOW ME BY NOW YOU HAVEN'T BEEN PAYING ATTENTION. I'M STEVE, AND I'LL BE THE FACILITATOR FOR YOUR GROUP.

WELL, YOU PICKED THE BEST GROUP! WE NEARLY WON THE VOLLEYBALL TOURNAMENT!

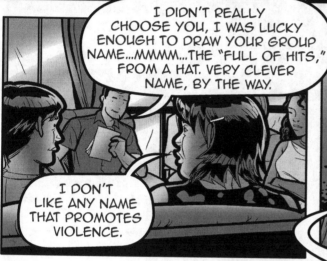

I DIDN'T REALLY CHOOSE YOU, I WAS LUCKY ENOUGH TO DRAW YOUR GROUP NAME...MMMM...THE "FULL OF HITS," FROM A HAT. VERY CLEVER NAME, BY THE WAY.

I DON'T LIKE ANY NAME THAT PROMOTES VIOLENCE.

ANYWAY, I HOPE YOU ALL HAD A GOOD TIME YESTERDAY.

I THOUGHT THE POOL PARTY WAS PARTICULARLY FUN. WHAT DID YOU ALL THINK?

YEAH, I HAD A GOOD TIME! ME AND MASON MET A TON OF PEOPLE.

MASON AND I?

YOU WEREN'T EVEN THERE.

16

OK, THEN. TODAY WE ARE GOING TO SPEND A LITTLE TIME GETTING TO KNOW ONE ANOTHER A LITTLE BETTER.

BASICALLY, I WANT US TO SHARE A LITTLE BIT ABOUT OUR VARIOUS BACKGROUNDS AND THEN DISCUSS OUR GOALS FOR THE FUTURE.

SO, WHO WANTS TO GO FIRST? HOW ABOUT YOU, MASON?

TELL US YOUR NAME, WHERE YOU ARE FROM, YOUR MAJOR, AND WHY YOU CHOSE THIS UNIVERSITY.

WHO, ME? UMMM, WELL, MY NAME IS MASON CARVER.

I'M FROM FAIRFIELD. I'M MAJORING IN ARCHITECTURE.

I CHOSE TO COME HERE BECAUSE IT HAS A GOOD ARCHITECTURE PROGRAM.

WOW, ARCHITECTURE. THAT'S HARD TO GET INTO.

YEAH, RIGHT NOW I'VE GOT THIS PROBLEM WITH MY SCHEDULE...

OH, MAN, GET THAT FIXED RIGHT AWAY. I MISSED A PREREQUISITE MY FRESHMAN YEAR AND IT PUT ME A YEAR BEHIND! ANYTHING ELSE?

YOU JUST HERE FOR THE ARCHITECTURE?

WE'LL IT'S FAIRLY CLOSE TO HOME, BUT NOT TOO CLOSE, IF YOU KNOW WHAT I MEAN.

I THINK WE ALL KNOW WHAT YOU MEAN, MASON. WHOSE NEXT?

GUESS THAT'S ME. I'M TRAVIS. I AM FROM CLAYTON.

I CAME HERE FOR A FOOTBALL SCHOLARSHIP. COACH BLEVINS IS AWESOME, AND I AM REAL GLAD TO BE HERE.

WHAT'S YOUR MAJOR, TRAVIS?

WELL, I HAVEN'T REALLY DECIDED YET. I AM JUST TAKING THE BASICS FOR NOW.

YOU KNOW THE BASICS LIKE WEIGHT LIFTING, JOGGING, AND FOOD AND NUTRITION.

I THINK I HAVE SOMETHING ELSE TOO. MAYBE SOMETHING I DON'T NEED, LIKE MATH?

HI, EVERYONE...AGAIN! I'M HEATHER AND I COME FROM ARLINGTON. BOTH OF MY PARENTS CAME HERE FOR COLLEGE. MY MOM WAS A LEGACY IN HER SORORITY, SO I REALLY DIDN'T HAVE MUCH CHOICE, DID I?

BUT I'M REALLY EXCITED TO BE HERE, FINALLY! OHHH...AND I'M A MARKETING MAJOR.

I'M MCALISTER CASTAS FROM SANTA FE. I DON'T KNOW WHAT I WANT TO MAJOR IN, BUT THIS SEEMED LIKE A COOL COLLEGE TOWN.

WELL, I AM ESTER TOMAS, ORIGINALLY FROM DENVER, BUT WHEN MY MOM GOT A NEW JOB, WE MOVED TO RIVERSIDE - BEEN THERE FOR ABOUT THREE YEARS.

I AM DEFINITELY MAJORING IN SOCIAL WORK. I CHOSE TO COME TO SCHOOL HERE BECAUSE OF THE MANY OPPORTUNITIES FOR SERVICE LEARNING I READ ABOUT ONLINE.

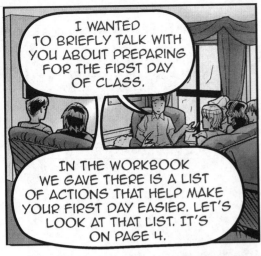

I WANTED TO BRIEFLY TALK WITH YOU ABOUT PREPARING FOR THE FIRST DAY OF CLASS.

IN THE WORKBOOK WE GAVE THERE IS A LIST OF ACTIONS THAT HELP MAKE YOUR FIRST DAY EASIER. LET'S LOOK AT THAT LIST. IT'S ON PAGE 4.

WHAT? NOBODY BROUGHT THEIR WORKBOOK? FINE, I'LL JUST READ THEM TO YOU. IF YOU HAVE A QUESTION, RAISE YOUR HAND.

ONE. GET YOUR TEXTBOOKS EARLY AND PREVIEW THEM BEFORE CLASS.

EXCUSE ME, BUT CAN WE ORDER TEXTBOOKS ONLINE? THEY ARE MUCH LESS EXPENSIVE.

SPACE CAMP

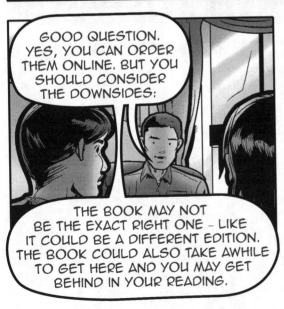

GOOD QUESTION. YES, YOU CAN ORDER THEM ONLINE. BUT YOU SHOULD CONSIDER THE DOWNSIDES:

THE BOOK MAY NOT BE THE EXACT RIGHT ONE - LIKE IT COULD BE A DIFFERENT EDITION. THE BOOK COULD ALSO TAKE AWHILE TO GET HERE AND YOU MAY GET BEHIND IN YOUR READING.

ALSO, REMEMBER TO KEEP YOUR RECEIPTS NO MATTER WHERE YOU GET YOUR BOOKS IN CASE YOU DROP A CLASS!

FOUR. LOCATE YOUR CLASSROOMS AND YOUR PROFESSORS' OFFICES BEFORE THE FIRST DAY.

MAKE SURE YOU KNOW HOW TO QUICKLY GET AROUND CAMPUS TO AVOID BEING LATE.

EVERYBODY CLEAR ON THOSE SUGGESTIONS? WE WILL HAVE ANOTHER MEETING LIKE THIS ONE IN A FEW DAYS - THE DAY BEFORE CLASSES START - TO COVER SOME BASIC ISSUES FOR THE FIRST DAY OF CLASS.

UNTIL THEN, I SUGGEST YOU TAKE CARE OF SOME OF THOSE ISSUES WE DISCUSSED. WE WILL MEET BACK IN THIS SAME SPOT NEXT TIME. SEE YOU THEN, IF NOT BEFORE!

THERE'S A FRESHMAN SOCIAL AT THE COMMONS TONIGHT.

RIGHT.

SURE.

I'VE GOT TO HEAD OVER TO CENTRAL CAMPUS.

IS THE STUDENT UNION THAT WAY? I WANT TO GET MY ID AND BUS PASS. MAYBE I'LL EVEN PICK UP ONE OF MY TEXTBOOKS IF IT'S IN COMIC FORMAT OR OTHERWISE INTRIGUING.

SURE. TRAVIS, YOU COMING?

YEAH, I'LL GO.

JUST A SEC. I'LL CATCH UP WITH YOU LATER. IT'S ONE OF THE GUYS FROM THE TEAM.

WHAT UP, T? THIS IS WHAT COLLEGE IS ALL ABOUT - RIGHT? HAVE A BEER.

UH...ALRIGHT.

HEY, KID, I CAN SEE YOU'RE MORE UNLUCKY THAN ANYTHING ELSE. YOU SHOULD PROBABLY CALL YOUR FOLKS AND HAVE THEM COME BAIL YOU OUT.

UH, THEY LIVE ABOUT 500 MILES FROM HERE. ARE THERE ANY OTHER OPTIONS?

WELL, DO YOU KNOW ANYONE LOCAL?

HELLO, THAT YOU MASON?? BRO, I NEED SOME HELP!

OK. GIVE ME A FEW MINUTES.

OH, AND CAN YOU BRING $300?

WHERE AM I SUPPOSED TO GET $300 IN THE MIDDLE OF THE NIGHT?

THE ATM, OF COURSE! THEN, YOU HAVE TO TAKE THE MONEY TO THE BAIL BOND GUY NEXT TO THE JAIL. YOU CAN JUST STOP ON YOUR WAY IN. I PROMISE I'LL PAY YOU BACK.

GEE, THANKS FOR THE CONVENIENCE.

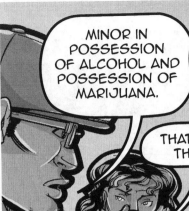

MINOR IN POSSESSION OF ALCOHOL AND POSSESSION OF MARIJUANA.

ANYWAY, THOSE ARE SERIOUS CHARGES, BUT I GUESS THAT'S WHAT HAPPENS WHEN YOU HANG WITH THOSE FOOTBALL PLAYERS.

I'M GLAD I DIDN'T GO WITH HIM!

THAT EXPLAINS THE SMELL!

ME TOO! WE MADE A GOOD CALL THERE!

WHY FOOTBALL IS SUCH A BIG DEAL AT COLLEGES IS BEYOND...

WELL, I'M PRETTY STRESSED OUT AND CLASSES HAVEN'T EVEN STARTED.

YOU KNOW, I WAS LOOKING THROUGH THAT FRESHMAN WORKBOOK YESTERDAY. IT HAS A CHAPTER ON STRESS MANAGEMENT.

COME ON! I'M NOT ABOUT TO FLIP OUT COMPLETELY...

ANYTHING TO KEEP YOU FROM OPENING A BOOK, RIGHT?

I SKIMMED IT TOO AND IT DID HAVE SOME GOOD IDEAS. LIKE TALKING WITH FRIENDS ABOUT YOUR PROBLEMS. BUT I GUESS MAYBE NOT YOUR POT-SMOKING FOOTBALL FRIENDS.

ACTUALLY, YOU ARE TALKING WITH US RIGHT NOW. ALSO, MAKING SURE YOU GET SOME EXERCISE EVERY DAY.

UH, HE'S ON THE FOOTBALL TEAM.

WE COULD PLAY CRICKET! THAT WOULD BE BETTER THAN JUST KICKING A BALL AROUND.

I FEEL REALLY STRESSED IF I DON'T GET ENOUGH COFFEE.

JUST HAVING THIS CUP IN MY HAND MAKES ME FEEL BETTER ABOUT TRAVIS'S SITUATION ALREADY.

YOU SHOULD ALSO GET PLENTY OF SLEEP. THAT'S PROBABLY YOUR MAIN PROBLEM

HARD TIME TAKES A TOLL ON THOSE KINDS OF THINGS, HUH, TRAVIS?

I GET AT LEAST NINE HOURS OF SLEEP - IT'S VERY IMPORTANT.

SO, WHAT DID EVERYONE ELSE DO LAST NIGHT?

THE DORM SOCIAL WAS ACTUALLY PRETTY FUN. I MOSTLY TALKED TO SOME OTHER SORORITY PLEDGES.

BY THE WAY, TODAY IS BID DAY, WHICH MEANS THE END OF RUSH - AND ALL MY RUSHING AROUND.

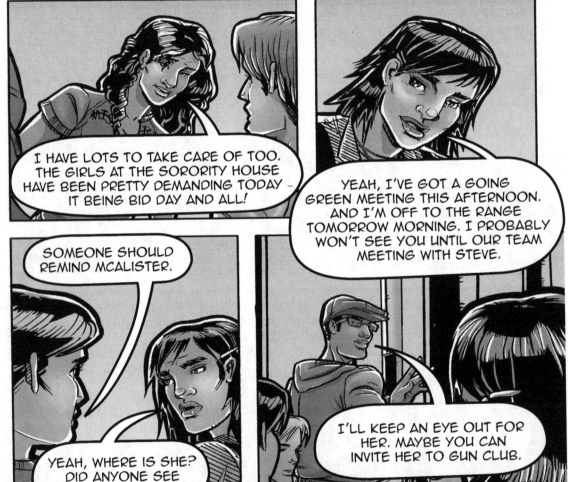

HI, HEATHER!

HI! SORRY, I'M RUNNING A LITTLE LATE. I FINALLY FOUND EVERYTHING ON THE LIST YOU GAVE ME FOR THE BID PARTY TONIGHT. WHAT DO YOU THINK?

HA, HA! YOU ACTUALLY FOUND A RUBBER CHICKEN?? THAT MIGHT BE A FIRST.

YES, THAT AND A DANNY ZUKO WIG. I DIDN'T EVEN KNOW WHO DANNY ZUKO WAS... THANK GOODNESS FOR THE INTERNET!

SERIOUSLY? TELL ME YOU DIDN'T ACTUALLY FALL FOR THAT GAG. YOU ALREADY GOT YOUR BID!

BUT YOU SAID IT WAS VERY IMPORTANT FOR THE BID PARTY TONIGHT...

WELL, NOW THAT ALL OF THAT IMPORTANT SCAVENGING WORK IS DONE, LET'S GO!

16

HEY, MOM.

NO, I'M OK. I JUST NEED TO CHECK ON SOMETHING. REMEMBER WHEN YOU WERE GOING TO PAY MY TUITION A FEW WEEKS AGO?

MASON...OH MY GOSH!! WHAT'S WRONG?!? ARE YOU HURT??

YES, I DO! BUT THEN YOU SAID YOU GOT A SCHOLARSHIP SO I THOUGHT THAT MEANT YOU DIDN'T HAVE TO PAY ANYTHING.

SOMEHOW I KNEW THAT'S WHAT YOU WERE GOING TO SAY...

21

OH, HI, MASON. I'M JUST TRYING TO GET ORGANIZED FOR CLASSES.

HEY, MCALISTER! WHAT'S GOING ON?

PLUS, STEVE SAYS IT'S IMPORTANT TO ORGANIZE MY CALENDAR. HERE IS NEXT WEEK'S SCHEDULE. BUT IT'S NOT FINISHED YET.

REALLY? ALREADY? IT TOOK ME ALL DAY JUST TO GET MY CLASSES FINALLY SETTLED UP.

YEAH, BEING REALLY ORGANIZED KEEPS ME FROM BEING STRESSED. I KNOW, I'M A HUGE NERD.

Weekly Planner

Monday:

8am.–9am.:

GET ORGANIZED!!!!

Tuesday:

7am.–8am.: OFF

8am.–11am.: Flextime

11am.–12pm.: Lunch

1pm.–2pm.: (See Steve) ♡

2pm.–3pm.: Dorm Meeting

Wednesday:

7am.–8am.: Breakfast and get to class

8am.–9am.: Biology

9am.–10am.: Study Time

10am.–11am.: Poli-Sci

11am.–12pm.: Lunch

2p.m.–3pm.: Biology Lab

Thursday:

7am.–8am.: Breakfast and get to class

8am.–10am.: History

10am.–11am.: Study Time

11am.–12pm.: Spanish

12p.m.–1pm.: Lunch

Friday:

7am.–8am.: Breakfast and get to class

8am.–9am.: Biology

9am.–10am.: Study Time

10am.–11am.: Poli-Sci

11am.–12pm.: Lunch

2p.m.–3pm.: Biology Lab

Saturday:

7am.–8am.: Breakfast and get to class

8am.–11am.: Flextime

1pm.–2pm.:

Laundry!!!

Sunday:

Call Mom back.

STEVE SUGGESTED I TRY TO BLOCK OFF TIMES AND STICK TO THEM, IF POSSIBLE. I AM REALLY WORRIED ABOUT SCHOOL – I HAVEN'T ALWAYS GOTTEN THE BEST GRADES.

STEVE SAYS ALL THAT, HUH? DID HE RECOMMEND THE UNICORN STICKERS TOO?

MY LITTLE SISTER GAVE ME THESE.

UH, I FEEL LIKE A JERK NOW.

I'M TOTALLY KIDDING. UNICORNS ROCK.

ANOTHER TRICK IS TO CREATE FLEXIBLE TIME AND USE THAT TIME TO TRADE OFF WITH OTHER ACTIVITIES IF YOU GET BEHIND. STEVE REALLY IS PRETTY SMART!

YEAH...HE SURE SEEMS TO HAVE IMPRESSED YOU. YOU KNOW WHO COULD STAND TO BE A LITTLE MORE ORGANIZED – TRAVIS. HE'S A SLOB...OUR ROOM IS ALREADY A MESS. HE HAS HIS STUFF EVERYWHERE, INCLUDING MY DRAWERS AND CLOSET.

WELL, I COULD SHOW YOU AROUND NOW THAT I KNOW WHERE EVERYTHING IS.

AND I CAN SHOW YOU WHERE ALL THE COFFEE SHOPS ARE. THAT'S ALWAYS THE FIRST THING I SCOUT OUT ANYWHERE NEW.

I KNOW A QUIET COFFEE SHOP THAT HAS LIVE MUSIC ON THE WEEKENDS.

GREAT, IT'S A DATE.

PLEASE, DO COME IN! BETTER LATE THAN NEVER. RIGHT, MR. ??????

UMMM...HELTER. SORRY...I...ERRR... COULDN'T FIND THE ROOM.

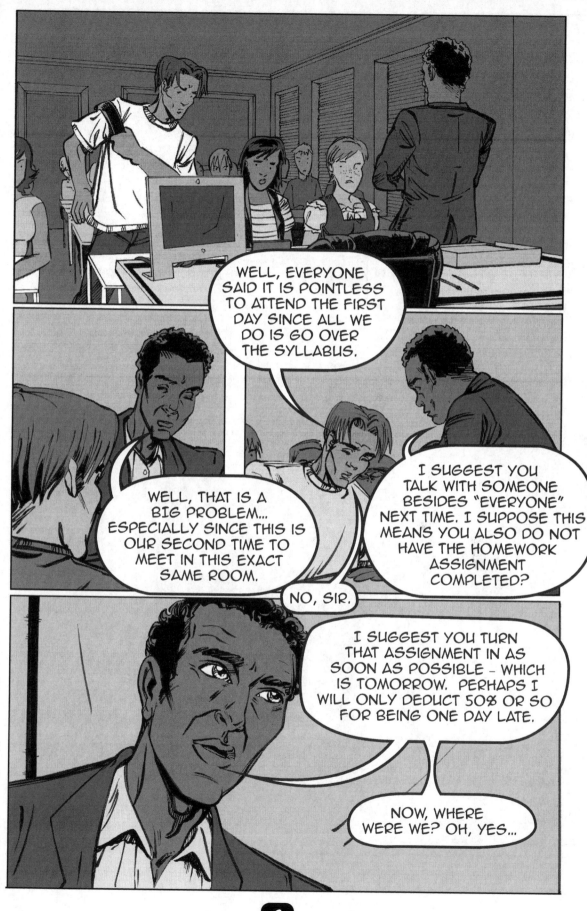

WELL, EVERYONE SAID IT IS POINTLESS TO ATTEND THE FIRST DAY SINCE ALL WE DO IS GO OVER THE SYLLABUS.

WELL, THAT IS A BIG PROBLEM... ESPECIALLY SINCE THIS IS OUR SECOND TIME TO MEET IN THIS EXACT SAME ROOM.

I SUGGEST YOU TALK WITH SOMEONE BESIDES "EVERYONE" NEXT TIME. I SUPPOSE THIS MEANS YOU ALSO DO NOT HAVE THE HOMEWORK ASSIGNMENT COMPLETED?

NO, SIR.

I SUGGEST YOU TURN THAT ASSIGNMENT IN AS SOON AS POSSIBLE - WHICH IS TOMORROW. PERHAPS I WILL ONLY DEDUCT 50% OR SO FOR BEING ONE DAY LATE.

NOW, WHERE WERE WE? OH, YES...

WELL I WOULDN'T DO IT AGAIN IF I WERE YOU. ESPECIALLY IF YOU SIT NEXT TO MCALISTER AND ME.

MCALISTER? OH, HEY, I DIDN'T SEE YOU IN CLASS.

NOT SURPRISING. I WAS ONLY SITTING THREE SEATS AWAY.

SEE YA, ESTER, I'VE GOT TO BE AT ALGEBRA IN 10 MINUTES. AND UNLIKE TRAVIS, THEY WILL NOTICE IF I'M NOT THERE.

OK, LET'S MEET UP LATER. I FOUND A REALLY GOOD FREE TRADE SMOOTHIE PLACE.

OHHH. THERE HE IS... PLAYING THE GUITAR. I DIDN'T KNOW HE PLAYED GUITAR. I'M IMPRESSED - HE MIGHT BE BOYFRIEND MATERIAL AFTER ALL.

THANKS FOR COMING WITH ME, LAST MINUTE.

I THOUGHT YOU SAID YOU WEREN'T INTERESTED IN HAVING A BOYFRIEND.

WHEN YOU TOLD ME THAT MASON WAS PLAYING....

AT THE GAME...

AREN'T YOU READY TO GO? ALL THE GIRLS ARE ALREADY AT THE HOUSE.

YOU'RE NOT SERIOUS? LESS THAN A MINUTE TO GO AND WE'RE ABOUT TO SCORE! THAT WOULD WIN THE GAME.

IT'S BEEN LESS THAN A MINUTE FOR ABOUT 20 MINUTES! THIS IS SO BORING!

TIGERS LINE UP. FIRST AND 10 ON THE 36-YARD LINE. DOUBLE WIDE OUT. ELLIOT DROPS BACK...LOOKS LEFT...

FIRES....IT'S CAUGHT! FABULOUS CATCH BY NUMBER 84, DORSEY, FOR A 12-YARD GAIN.

THE CROWD GOES WILD! YOU COULDN'T HAVE ASKED FOR A MORE EXCITING FIRST GAME OF THE SEASON!

WE COULD ACTUALLY WIN THIS!

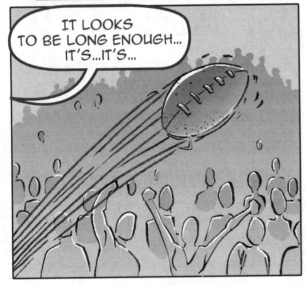

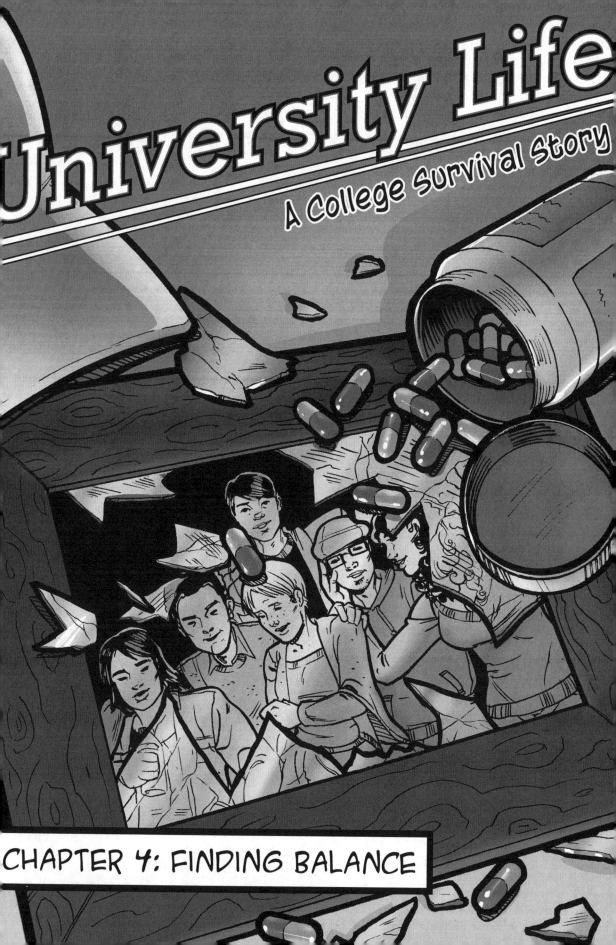

WELBY DORM

BLEEEEP, BLEEEEP BLEEEEP

THESE 8 O'CLOCK CLASSES ARE GOING TO KILL ME...

WHAAA? HUH?

WHAT IS WRONG WITH YOU SETTING AN ALARM NOW? THIS IS SATURDAY! NOW SHUT UP AND LET ME GET SOME SLEEP!

GOOD LUCK WITH THAT! HAVE YOU EVER EVEN HAD A JOB?

NO, BUT HOW HARD CAN IT BE?

YOU MIGHT BE SURPRISED... IT'S NOT THAT EASY TO BALANCE JOB AND SCHOOL, WHILE STILL HAVING A SOCIAL LIFE.

I GUESS I DON'T HAVE MUCH OF A CHOICE. MY DAD WAS SO PISSED! HE IS MAKING ME DEVELOP A BUDGET TOO. I DON'T REALLY EVEN KNOW WHAT A BUDGET IS!

DOES THAT MEAN I CAN ONLY BUY THINGS THAT ARE ON SALE?

MAYBE YOU COULD CHECK WITH THE FINANCIAL AID OFFICE OR LOOK FOR AN INTERNSHIP? YOUR DAD MIGHT BE MORE FORGIVING IF YOU GET AN INTERNSHIP - PAID OR NOT.

WELL, THAT'S GOOD FOOD FOR THOUGHT.

UM, SO I SHOULD PROBABLY GO BEFORE THIS GETS AWKWARD. SEE YA AROUND?

YEAH. SEE YA.

HELLO?

MOM? HI.

MASON, IS EVERYTHING ALRIGHT? WHAT'S GOT YOU UP SO EARLY ON A SATURDAY?

EVERYTHING IS FINE.

REMEMBER WHEN YOU WERE SEVEN AND USED TO GET UP SOOO EARLY JUST TO WATCH THE BLUE POWER RANGER?

NOT REALLY.

WHAT'S WRONG, SWEETHEART? YOU SOUND DOWN.

HELLO?

UHHH, ESTER. THAT YOU? THIS IS STEVE HARDING, YOUR RA.

JUST A SEC, STEVE. I'M ON THE TREADMILL.

SORRY, STEVE. TRYING TO GET SOME EXERCISE. YOU KNOW WHAT THEY SAY,

"HEALTHY BODY, HEALTHY MIND."

GOOD FOR YOU...

APPARENTLY, SHE LISTED ME AS HER EMERGENCY CONTACT NUMBER BUT I DON'T REALLY KNOW WHY.

I THINK SHE HAS CLOSER FRIENDS THAN ME.

UH, NO.

OH, MAN! THAT'S AWFUL. I MEAN. WELL, THAT MIGHT EXPLAIN SOME THINGS.

WHY?

AREN'T YOU GUYS DATING?

FOR ONE, IT SEEMS SHE HAD HOPED THAT YOU TWO MIGHT START DATING.

AND CLEARLY THAT'S NOT HAPPENING.

I HAD NO IDEA.

AND SHE'S BEEN REALLY WITHDRAWN RECENTLY. I THOUGHT SHE WAS SPENDING TIME WITH YOU.

OH, I HAVEN'T SEEN HER AT ANY OF THE FUNCTIONS RECENTLY. ANYWAY, I THOUGHT MAYBE YOU WOULD GO TALK TO HER?

SHE'S AT UNIVERSITY HOSPITAL.

I'LL GO SEE HER RIGHT AWAY. THANKS FOR CALLING. BYE!

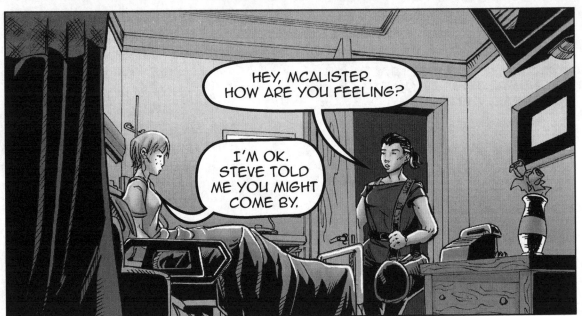

SO, A BUNCH OF US ARE A PART OF A DISASTER RELIEF ACTIVIST GROUP KNOWN AS DISASTER INVOLVEMENT AND EMERGENCY SUPPORT.

DIES?!? REALLY? YOU SHOULD PROBABLY CHANGE THE NAME OF YOUR GROUP.

IN RETROSPECT, THAT'S A GOOD IDEA.

WHO'S THAT LADY? I DON'T RECOGNIZE HER.

THAT'S DEBBIE. SHE'S A SINGLE MOTHER OF THREE, AND SHE HAS A 4.0.

ANYWAY, THE GROUP WENT THROUGH A ROPES COURSE AS A TEAM-BUILDING EXERCISE.

WOW. CURVEBUSTER MOM!

HERE'S ANOTHER... OF ME.

HEE HEE... OH, SORRY, YOU JUST LOOK SO SCARED. ARE ROPES COURSES SCARY?

NOT REALLY...WELL, MAYBE AT FIRST. MOVING ON...

THAT MAKES SENSE...

OUR CLUB'S FACULTY ADVISOR, DR. SHERRIDAN - THAT'S HER THERE - THOUGHT

THAT GOING THROUGH THE ROPES COURSE WOULD BE A GOOD WAY TO DEVELOP CAMARADERIE.

SHE SAID THAT TEAMWORK WAS VERY IMPORTANT IN TODAY'S WORK ENVIRONMENT,

AND IT IS IMPORTANT TO LEARN HOW TO INTERACT WITH A DIVERSE GROUP OF PEOPLE, ESPECIALLY THOSE FROM OTHER CULTURES.

NOT REALLY. I HAVE BEEN HAVING A REALLY HARD TIME LATELY FINDING MY BALANCE.

I HAVE HAD TO LEARN TO SAY "NO" - WHICH IS EXTREMELY HARD FOR ME.

BALANCE. THAT'S GOING TO BE MY NEW MANTRA.

THAT IS EASY FOR YOU TO SAY. YOU ALWAYS HAVE IT SO "TOGETHER"!

SOUNDS LIKE A GOOD PLAN.

SERIOUSLY, ESTER. THANKS FOR COMING. YOU'RE A GOOD FRIEND!

YOU'RE WELCOME.

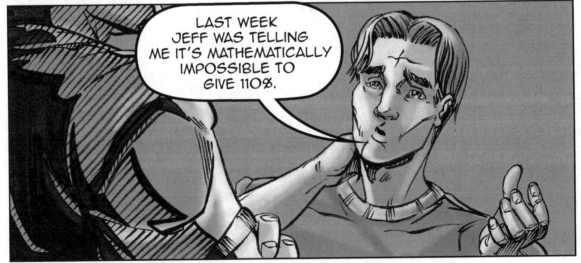

YOU THERE, FRESHMAN BACK-UP KICKER!

YES, SIR?

GO RUN THE BLEACHERS WITH HELTER - AND KEEP ACCURATE

COUNT! YOU FIND A WAY FOR HIM TO GIVE ME 110%.

TRAVIS?

YEAH?

YOU SUCK!

University Life

A College Survival Story

CHAPTER FIVE: REFLECTIONS

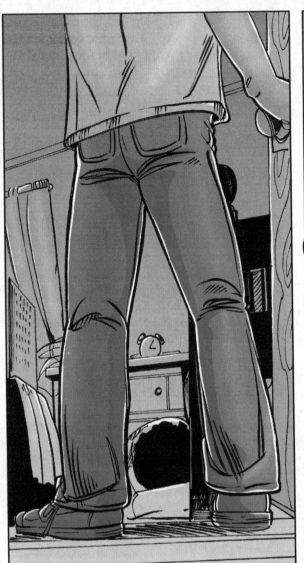

YO, MASON! YOU ASLEEP??

MASON! WAKE UP!

HUH?

GET UP OFF THE FLOOR, MAN! DID YOU FORGET OUR MEETING?

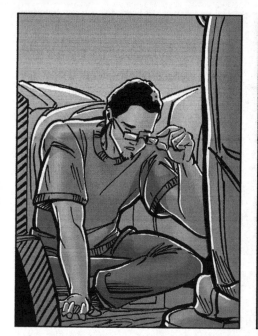

I WAS SLEEPING... FINALLY. WHAT GIVES?

WE ARE HAVING OUR FINAL SMALL GROUP MEETING RIGHT NOW. YOU ARE THE ONLY ONE NOT THERE - I JUST CAME TO LOOK FOR YOU.

OH, YEAH. TOTALLY FORGOT ABOUT THAT - IT'S NOT ON THE TOP OF MY PRIORITY LIST RIGHT NOW.

WHERE HAVE YOU BEEN ANYWAY? I HAVEN'T SEEN YOU IN A COUPLE OF DAYS.

BEEN WORKING ON MY FINAL ARCHITECTURE PROJECT - IT'S DUE THIS AFTERNOON.

OHH. SO, TO CELEBRATE YOU DECIDED TO SLEEP ON THE FLOOR?

I DON'T REALLY REMEMBER GOING TO SLEEP – I MUST HAVE JUST PASSED OUT...

PULLED TWO ALL-NIGHTERS BACK TO BACK.

YOU DO REMEMBER WE HAD CHICKENS IN THIS ROOM AT ONE TIME?

HOW COULD I FORGET.

JEEZ...I WOULDN'T EVEN SLEEP ON OUR FLOOR!

HEE HEE! YOUR ROOM IS THE BEST.

I BET TRAVIS STILL HAS PICTURES OF DAVID HASSELHOFF ON THE WALLS. REMEMBER WHEN SOMEONE PUT NAKED PICTURES OF HASSELHOFF ALL OVER THE ROOM?

HE WASN'T NAKED! BESIDES, "THE HOFF" WORKED WITH SOME HOT GIRLS BACK IN THE BAYWATCH DAYS!

WHATEVER, DUDE. YOU WEREN'T EVEN BORN THEN!

SO!?! THOSE GIRLS WERE STILL HOT...

WELL...I CAN START, I GUESS. EVERYONE HERE PRETTY MUCH KNOWS MY PROBLEMS ANYWAY.

WHAT CREATED THIS CHALLENGE?

MY CHALLENGE HAS BEEN WITH MONEY AND, NOW, WITH MANAGING A JOB AND SCHOOL.

A LITTLE?

I RACKED UP SOME DEBT QUICKLY - MOSTLY BY BUYING THINGS I DIDN'T REALLY NEED. AND I GOT MYSELF IN A LITTLE TROUBLE WITH CREDIT CARDS.

MAYBE MORE THAN A LITTLE. ENOUGH THAT MY FATHER HAD TO BAIL ME OUT, BUT ON THE CONDITION I FIND A JOB AND PAY HIM BACK FULLY.

FINDING A JOB WAS HARDER THAN I THOUGHT. TURNS OUT THAT NOT MANY PEOPLE WANT TO HIRE SOMEONE WITH NO EXPERIENCE.

SO, TELL ME ABOUT YOUR PREVIOUS WORK EXPERIENCE?

I FINALLY FOUND A JOB AT JAZZY JOE'S AS A BARISTA.

I SEEM TO REMEMBER SOMEONE, AHHH ME, MENTIONING JAZZY JOE'S FROM THE OUTSET.

ANYWAY, I'VE LEARNED A LOT ABOUT BUSINESS AND DEALING WITH PEOPLE.

I HAVE A NEW RESPECT FOR PEOPLE WHO WORK IN THE FOOD AND BEVERAGE SERVICES.

I PLAN ON KEEPING THE JOB AT JJ'S – TURNS OUT, I HAVE MADE SOME REALLY GOOD FRIENDS THERE.

CLOSED

THE WHOLE SITUATION HAS FORCED ME TO MANAGE MY TIME BETTER, AND I AM PROUD THAT I HELD DOWN A JOB AND FINISHED THE SEMESTER WITH PRETTY GOOD GRADES.

AT FIRST, I THOUGHT TO STUDY HARD AND MAKE EXCELLENT GRADES WAS BEST.

BUT I LEARNED THAT I AM HAPPIER WITH FRIENDS, NOT JUST SPENDING TIME ONLINE TALKING TO FRIENDS FROM PUNE. ONLINE NETWORKING IS NO SUBSTITUTE FOR FACE-TO-FACE RELATIONSHIPS.

SO, WHILE HERE, I TRY TO MAKE MANY NEW FRIENDS. I FOUND THAT IT IS IMPORTANT TO ASK QUESTIONS, LISTEN TO OTHERS, AND SHOW INTEREST IN THE OTHER PEOPLE TO DEVELOP NEW RELATIONSHIPS.

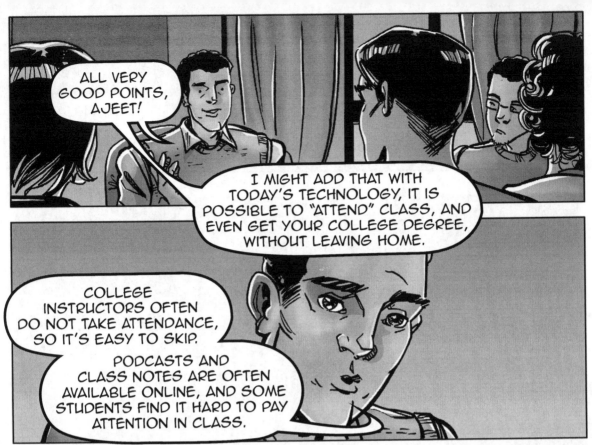

I'LL GO.

PROBABLY THE MOST CHALLENGING PART OF THIS SEMESTER IS DEALING WITH THE DEMANDS OF COLLEGE, WHILE PLAYING BALL.

COACH AND MY TEAMMATES DEMAND MY VERY BEST DURING PRACTICE AND THE GAMES. I JUST SEEM TO BE TIRED A LOT!

SINCE THEN, I HAVE TRIED TO BE MORE EFFICIENT. I'VE DISCOVERED THAT I HAVE A TENDENCY TO JUST WASTE TIME.

THE FIRST FEW WEEKS OF THE SEMESTER WERE A BIG WAKE-UP CALL FOR ME.

I WOULDN'T CALL REDECORATING YOUR DORM ROOM WALLS WITH HOFF ART A WASTE OF TIME...

I DON'T CLAIM THAT ONE, OF COURSE, BUT I MIGHT HAVE PARTICIPATED

WHEN STEVE'S ROOM WAS FILLED WITH INFLATED LATEX GLOVES.

THAT WAS YOU?!? IF I HAD KNOWN... I WOULD HAVE...

ANYWAY... I HAVE WORKED TO IMPROVE MY STUDY HABITS BY STUDYING REGULARLY WITH A GROUP AND

BY REMOVING DISTRACTIONS. LIKE MY CELL PHONE, I JUST TURN IT OFF NOW WHILE I AM STUDYING.

I AM HAPPY TO REPORT THAT I FOUND OUT THIS MORNING THAT I MADE A 68 ON MY FINAL POLITICAL SCIENCE EXAM AND PASSED THE COURSE!

SPECIAL THANKS TO ESTER AND MCALISTER FOR BEING SUCH GREAT STUDY PARTNERS!

AWESOME NEWS, TRAVIS! YOU TURNED OUT TO BE A PRETTY GOOD STUDY PARTNER AS WELL.

I ALSO LEARNED A LOT FROM YOUR ESSAY ON "DRUG USE AND THE MIRANDA WARNING."

YOU HAD SOME REALLY UNIQUE INSIGHTS IN THAT PAPER!

TRAVIS, HOW IN THE WORLD DID YOU GET IN MY ROOM? I CAN'T SEE...

UMM, EXCUSE ME STEVE, YOU WANT ME TO GO NEXT?

ERRR, YES, I SUPPOSE.

MY PRIMARY CHALLENGE THIS SEMESTER HAS DEVELOPED BECAUSE I WAS TAKING ON TOO MANY RESPONSIBILITIES.

AT ONE TIME, I WAS INVOLVED IN IN SIX DIFFERENT CLUBS. I HAD LITTLE TIME JUST FOR ME.

SAVE the PORCUPINES

GUN CLUB

RECYCLE

VOTE

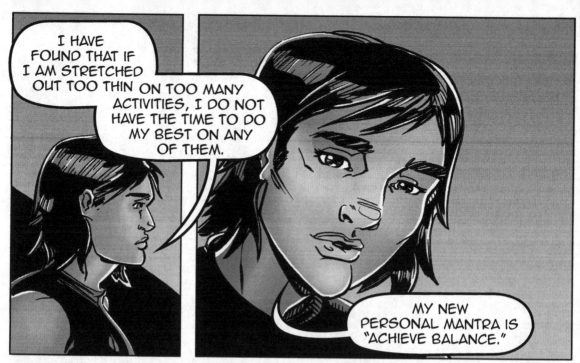

IN THE END, I DECIDED THAT A BIG UNIVERSITY ENVIRONMENT MAY NOT BE FOR ME.
FOR THE TIME BEING, I AM GOING TO MOVE CLOSER TO HOME AND ATTEND A COMMUNITY COLLEGE.

OH, MCALISTER, WHY DIDN'T YOU TELL ME? I WILL MISS YOU!

I WILL MISS YOU TOO! ACTUALLY, I WILL MISS ALL OF YOU HERE - THIS GROUP HAS BEEN THE BEST PART OF MY COLLEGE EXPERIENCE!

WITH THAT SAID, I AM GOING TO GO.

GO? YOU MEAN GO HOME RIGHT NOW??

YES, I DON'T WANT TO HAVE ANY EXTENDED, AWKWARD GOODBYES.

IF NO ONE ELSE IS GOING TO SAY IT, THEN I WILL! TIME FOR A GROUP HUG!